50 Budget-Friendly Meal Prep Recipes for Home

By: Kelly Johnson

Table of Contents

- Mediterranean Quinoa Salad
- Sausage and Pepper Foil Packets
- Tofu Vegetable Stir-Fry
- Spinach and Mushroom Quiche
- Turkey and Veggie Skillet
- Egg Roll in a Bowl
- Veggie Packed Bolognese Sauce
- Lemon Garlic Shrimp with Zucchini Noodles
- Chicken Caesar Salad Wraps
- Veggie and Chickpea Curry
- Turkey and Veggie Stir-Fry with Peanut Sauce
- Broccoli and Cheddar Stuffed Chicken Breasts
- Tomato Basil Zucchini Noodles
- Eggplant Rollatini
- Lentil Shepherd's Pie

Chicken and Vegetable Stir-Fry

Ingredients:

- 1 lb (450g) boneless, skinless chicken breasts, thinly sliced
- 2 tablespoons soy sauce
- 1 tablespoon rice vinegar
- 1 tablespoon sesame oil
- 2 cloves garlic, minced
- 1 teaspoon fresh ginger, minced
- 2 tablespoons vegetable oil, divided
- 1 onion, thinly sliced
- 1 bell pepper, thinly sliced
- 1 cup broccoli florets
- 1 carrot, julienned
- 1 cup snap peas
- Salt and pepper, to taste
- Cooked rice or noodles, for serving

Instructions:

In a small bowl, mix together soy sauce, rice vinegar, sesame oil, minced garlic, and minced ginger. Set aside.

Heat 1 tablespoon of vegetable oil in a large skillet or wok over medium-high heat. Add the sliced chicken and stir-fry until cooked through and browned, about 5-7 minutes. Remove the chicken from the skillet and set aside.

In the same skillet, add the remaining tablespoon of vegetable oil. Add the sliced onion, bell pepper, broccoli florets, julienned carrot, and snap peas. Stir-fry the vegetables until they are tender-crisp, about 5-7 minutes.

Return the cooked chicken to the skillet with the vegetables. Pour the prepared sauce over the chicken and vegetables, and toss everything together until evenly coated. Cook for an additional 2-3 minutes to heat through and allow the flavors to meld.

Season the stir-fry with salt and pepper to taste.

Serve the Chicken and Vegetable Stir-Fry hot over cooked rice or noodles.

Enjoy your delicious and nutritious Chicken and Vegetable Stir-Fry! Feel free to customize the vegetables according to your preferences, and adjust the seasonings to taste.

One-Pot Turkey Chili

Ingredients:

- 1 tablespoon olive oil
- 1 onion, diced
- 3 cloves garlic, minced
- 1 lb (450g) ground turkey
- 1 can (15 oz) kidney beans, drained and rinsed
- 1 can (15 oz) black beans, drained and rinsed
- 1 can (15 oz) diced tomatoes
- 1 can (6 oz) tomato paste
- 1 cup corn kernels (fresh, frozen, or canned)
- 2 cups chicken broth
- 1 tablespoon chili powder
- 1 teaspoon ground cumin
- 1 teaspoon dried oregano
- Salt and pepper to taste
- Optional toppings: shredded cheese, diced avocado, sour cream, chopped cilantro, sliced jalapeños, tortilla chips

Instructions:

Heat olive oil in a large pot over medium heat. Add diced onion and minced garlic, and cook until softened, about 3-4 minutes.
Add ground turkey to the pot, breaking it apart with a spoon, and cook until browned, about 5-6 minutes.
Stir in kidney beans, black beans, diced tomatoes, tomato paste, corn kernels, chicken broth, chili powder, ground cumin, and dried oregano.
Bring the chili to a simmer, then reduce the heat to low. Cover and let it simmer for 20-25 minutes, stirring occasionally.
Taste the chili and season with salt and pepper to taste.
Serve the One-Pot Turkey Chili hot, garnished with your favorite toppings such as shredded cheese, diced avocado, sour cream, chopped cilantro, sliced jalapeños, or tortilla chips.
Enjoy your delicious and comforting One-Pot Turkey Chili!

This recipe is perfect for busy weeknights because it's quick to make and requires only one pot for easy cleanup. Feel free to adjust the seasonings and ingredients according to your preferences, adding more or less chili powder for spiciness or additional vegetables for extra flavor and nutrition.

Spaghetti Squash with Tomato Sauce

Ingredients:

- 1 medium spaghetti squash
- 2 tablespoons olive oil
- Salt and pepper, to taste
- 2 cloves garlic, minced
- 1 can (14 oz) diced tomatoes
- 1 can (6 oz) tomato paste
- 1 teaspoon dried basil
- 1 teaspoon dried oregano
- 1/2 teaspoon dried thyme
- 1/2 teaspoon crushed red pepper flakes (optional)
- Grated Parmesan cheese, for serving
- Fresh basil leaves, for garnish (optional)

Instructions:

Preheat your oven to 400°F (200°C).

Cut the spaghetti squash in half lengthwise and scoop out the seeds and stringy pulp from the center.

Drizzle the cut sides of the spaghetti squash with olive oil and season with salt and pepper.

Place the spaghetti squash halves, cut side down, on a baking sheet lined with parchment paper or aluminum foil.

Roast the spaghetti squash in the preheated oven for 35-45 minutes, or until the flesh is tender and easily pierced with a fork.

While the spaghetti squash is roasting, prepare the tomato sauce. In a saucepan, heat olive oil over medium heat. Add minced garlic and cook until fragrant, about 1 minute.

Stir in diced tomatoes, tomato paste, dried basil, dried oregano, dried thyme, and crushed red pepper flakes (if using).

Bring the sauce to a simmer, then reduce the heat to low and let it simmer for 15-20 minutes, stirring occasionally, to allow the flavors to meld together.

Once the spaghetti squash is done roasting, remove it from the oven and let it cool slightly.

Use a fork to scrape the flesh of the spaghetti squash into strands.

Serve the spaghetti squash topped with tomato sauce and garnished with grated Parmesan cheese and fresh basil leaves, if desired.

Enjoy your delicious and healthy Spaghetti Squash with Tomato Sauce!

This dish is a nutritious and low-carb alternative to traditional pasta, and the tomato sauce adds plenty of flavor and zest. Feel free to customize the sauce with your favorite herbs and spices, or add cooked ground meat or vegetables for extra protein and texture.

Vegetable Fried Rice

Ingredients:

- 2 cups cooked white rice, cooled (day-old rice works best)
- 2 tablespoons vegetable oil
- 2 cloves garlic, minced
- 1 small onion, diced
- 2 carrots, diced
- 1 bell pepper, diced
- 1 cup frozen peas, thawed
- 2 eggs, lightly beaten
- 3 tablespoons soy sauce
- 1 tablespoon sesame oil
- Salt and pepper, to taste
- Optional garnish: sliced green onions, sesame seeds

Instructions:

Heat 1 tablespoon of vegetable oil in a large skillet or wok over medium-high heat.

Add minced garlic and diced onion to the skillet, and cook until softened and fragrant, about 2-3 minutes.

Add diced carrots and bell pepper to the skillet, and cook until vegetables are tender-crisp, about 3-4 minutes.

Push the vegetables to one side of the skillet, and add the beaten eggs to the empty side. Scramble the eggs until cooked through, then stir them into the vegetables.

Add the cooked rice and thawed peas to the skillet, and stir to combine with the vegetables and eggs.

Drizzle soy sauce and sesame oil over the rice mixture, and toss until everything is evenly coated.

Cook the fried rice for an additional 3-4 minutes, stirring occasionally, to allow the flavors to meld together.

Taste the fried rice and adjust seasoning with salt and pepper as needed.

Optional: Garnish the fried rice with sliced green onions and sesame seeds before serving.

Serve the Vegetable Fried Rice hot as a delicious and satisfying main dish or side dish.

Enjoy your homemade Vegetable Fried Rice! This versatile dish is perfect for using up leftover rice and vegetables, and you can customize it with your favorite veggies and protein sources such as tofu, shrimp, or chicken.

Turkey Meatball Subs

Ingredients:

For the meatballs:

- 1 lb (450g) ground turkey
- 1/2 cup breadcrumbs
- 1/4 cup grated Parmesan cheese
- 1 egg
- 2 cloves garlic, minced
- 1 teaspoon dried oregano
- 1 teaspoon dried basil
- Salt and pepper, to taste
- Olive oil, for cooking

For the subs:

- 4 sub rolls or hoagie buns
- 1 cup marinara sauce
- 1 cup shredded mozzarella cheese
- Fresh basil leaves, for garnish (optional)

Instructions:

Making the meatballs:

Preheat your oven to 400°F (200°C) and line a baking sheet with parchment paper.
In a large mixing bowl, combine the ground turkey, breadcrumbs, grated Parmesan cheese, egg, minced garlic, dried oregano, dried basil, salt, and pepper. Mix until well combined.
Shape the turkey mixture into meatballs, about 1 inch in diameter, and place them on the prepared baking sheet.
Drizzle the meatballs with olive oil and bake in the preheated oven for 20-25 minutes, or until cooked through and golden brown.

Assembling the subs:

While the meatballs are baking, heat the marinara sauce in a saucepan over medium heat until warmed through.
Slice the sub rolls or hoagie buns in half lengthwise, leaving one side attached.
Place a layer of meatballs on the bottom half of each roll. Spoon some marinara sauce over the meatballs, then sprinkle with shredded mozzarella cheese.

Return the subs to the oven and broil for 2-3 minutes, or until the cheese is melted and bubbly.
Remove the subs from the oven and garnish with fresh basil leaves, if desired.
Serve the Turkey Meatball Subs hot and enjoy!

These Turkey Meatball Subs are perfect for a satisfying lunch or dinner. Feel free to customize them with your favorite toppings such as sliced onions, bell peppers, or a sprinkle of red pepper flakes for extra heat.

Lentil Soup with Vegetables

Ingredients:

- 1 cup dried lentils, rinsed and drained
- 6 cups vegetable broth or water
- 2 tablespoons olive oil
- 1 onion, diced
- 2 carrots, diced
- 2 celery stalks, diced
- 3 cloves garlic, minced
- 1 teaspoon ground cumin
- 1 teaspoon ground coriander
- 1/2 teaspoon paprika
- 1 bay leaf
- Salt and pepper, to taste
- 1 can (14 oz) diced tomatoes
- 2 cups chopped spinach or kale
- 2 tablespoons lemon juice
- Fresh parsley, chopped, for garnish (optional)

Instructions:

In a large pot, heat the olive oil over medium heat. Add the diced onion, carrots, and celery, and cook until softened, about 5-7 minutes.

Add the minced garlic, ground cumin, ground coriander, paprika, and bay leaf to the pot. Cook for another 1-2 minutes, until fragrant.

Stir in the rinsed lentils and vegetable broth (or water) to the pot. Season with salt and pepper to taste.

Bring the soup to a boil, then reduce the heat to low and let it simmer, covered, for about 20-25 minutes, or until the lentils are tender.

Once the lentils are cooked, add the diced tomatoes (with their juices) and chopped spinach or kale to the pot. Cook for another 5 minutes, until the vegetables are heated through and the greens are wilted.

Remove the bay leaf from the soup and discard. Stir in the lemon juice, then taste and adjust seasoning if needed.

Ladle the Lentil Soup with Vegetables into bowls and garnish with fresh chopped parsley, if desired.

Serve the soup hot and enjoy!

This Lentil Soup with Vegetables is hearty, nutritious, and full of flavor. It's perfect for a comforting meal on a chilly day, and you can customize it with your favorite vegetables and herbs. Pair it with crusty bread or a side salad for a complete and satisfying meal.

Stuffed Bell Peppers

Ingredients:

- 4 large bell peppers (any color), halved and seeds removed
- 1 lb (450g) lean ground beef or turkey
- 1 cup cooked rice (white or brown)
- 1 small onion, diced
- 2 cloves garlic, minced
- 1 can (14 oz) diced tomatoes, drained
- 1 cup shredded cheese (cheddar, mozzarella, or your favorite)
- 1 tablespoon olive oil
- 1 teaspoon dried oregano
- 1 teaspoon dried basil
- Salt and pepper, to taste
- Fresh parsley or cilantro, chopped, for garnish (optional)

Instructions:

Preheat your oven to 375°F (190°C).

In a large skillet, heat the olive oil over medium heat. Add the diced onion and minced garlic, and cook until softened and fragrant, about 3-4 minutes.

Add the ground beef or turkey to the skillet, and cook until browned, breaking it apart with a spoon as it cooks.

Stir in the cooked rice, diced tomatoes, dried oregano, dried basil, salt, and pepper. Cook for another 2-3 minutes, until the mixture is heated through and well combined.

Remove the skillet from the heat and stir in half of the shredded cheese.

Place the bell pepper halves, cut side up, in a baking dish.

Spoon the beef and rice mixture evenly into each bell pepper half, pressing down gently to pack it in.

Cover the baking dish with aluminum foil and bake in the preheated oven for 25-30 minutes, or until the bell peppers are tender.

Remove the foil from the baking dish, sprinkle the remaining shredded cheese over the top of each stuffed bell pepper, and return to the oven. Bake for an additional 5 minutes, or until the cheese is melted and bubbly.

Remove the stuffed bell peppers from the oven and let them cool slightly before serving.

Garnish with chopped fresh parsley or cilantro, if desired.

Serve the Stuffed Bell Peppers hot and enjoy!

These Stuffed Bell Peppers are a delicious and satisfying meal that's easy to make and full of flavor. Feel free to customize the filling with your favorite ingredients such as quinoa, black beans, corn, or diced vegetables.

Quinoa Salad with Chickpeas and Veggies

Ingredients:

- 1 cup quinoa, rinsed
- 2 cups water or vegetable broth
- 1 can (15 oz) chickpeas, drained and rinsed
- 1 cup cherry tomatoes, halved
- 1 cucumber, diced
- 1 bell pepper, diced
- 1/4 cup red onion, finely chopped
- 1/4 cup fresh parsley, chopped
- 1/4 cup fresh cilantro, chopped (optional)
- 1/4 cup feta cheese, crumbled (optional)
- 1/4 cup sliced almonds or pine nuts (optional)

For the dressing:

- 1/4 cup olive oil
- 2 tablespoons lemon juice
- 1 tablespoon balsamic vinegar
- 1 clove garlic, minced
- 1 teaspoon Dijon mustard
- Salt and pepper, to taste

Instructions:

In a medium saucepan, combine the quinoa and water or vegetable broth. Bring to a boil, then reduce the heat to low, cover, and simmer for 15-20 minutes, or until the quinoa is cooked and the liquid is absorbed. Remove from heat and let it cool.

In a large salad bowl, combine the cooked quinoa, chickpeas, cherry tomatoes, cucumber, bell pepper, red onion, parsley, and cilantro (if using).

In a small bowl, whisk together the olive oil, lemon juice, balsamic vinegar, minced garlic, Dijon mustard, salt, and pepper to make the dressing.

Pour the dressing over the quinoa and vegetable mixture, and toss until everything is evenly coated.

If using, sprinkle the crumbled feta cheese and sliced almonds or pine nuts over the top of the salad.

Taste and adjust seasoning if needed.

Serve the Quinoa Salad with Chickpeas and Veggies chilled or at room temperature.
Enjoy your delicious and nutritious quinoa salad as a side dish or a light meal!

This Quinoa Salad with Chickpeas and Veggies is packed with protein, fiber, and nutrients, making it a healthy and satisfying option for lunch or dinner. Feel free to customize the salad with your favorite vegetables, herbs, and toppings, and adjust the dressing to your taste preferences.

Black Bean Tacos with Avocado

Ingredients:

- 1 can (15 oz) black beans, drained and rinsed
- 1 tablespoon olive oil
- 1 small onion, diced
- 2 cloves garlic, minced
- 1 teaspoon ground cumin
- 1 teaspoon chili powder
- Salt and pepper, to taste
- 8 small corn or flour tortillas
- 1 ripe avocado, sliced
- Salsa, for topping
- Fresh cilantro, chopped, for garnish (optional)
- Lime wedges, for serving

Instructions:

Heat olive oil in a skillet over medium heat. Add diced onion and minced garlic, and sauté until softened and fragrant, about 3-4 minutes.

Stir in the drained and rinsed black beans, ground cumin, chili powder, salt, and pepper. Cook for another 2-3 minutes, until the beans are heated through and well coated with the spices.

While the beans are cooking, warm the tortillas according to package instructions.

Spoon the black bean mixture onto each warm tortilla.

Top the tacos with sliced avocado, salsa, and chopped cilantro, if desired.

Serve the Black Bean Tacos with Avocado with lime wedges on the side for squeezing over the tacos.

Enjoy your delicious and nutritious tacos!

These Black Bean Tacos with Avocado are quick and easy to make, perfect for a weeknight dinner or a Meatless Monday meal. Feel free to customize the toppings to your liking, adding shredded lettuce, diced tomatoes, shredded cheese, or a dollop of sour cream. You can also use crunchy taco shells instead of soft tortillas if preferred.

Eggplant Parmesan

Ingredients:

- 2 medium eggplants, sliced into 1/2-inch rounds
- Salt, for sweating the eggplant
- 2 cups breadcrumbs (Italian seasoned breadcrumbs work well)
- 1 cup grated Parmesan cheese
- 2 eggs, beaten
- Olive oil, for frying
- 2 cups marinara sauce
- 2 cups shredded mozzarella cheese
- Fresh basil leaves, chopped, for garnish (optional)

Instructions:

Preheat your oven to 375°F (190°C).

Place the eggplant slices in a colander and sprinkle them generously with salt. Let them sit for about 30 minutes to release excess moisture. This step helps to reduce bitterness and improve the texture of the eggplant.

While the eggplant is sweating, prepare the breadcrumb mixture. In a shallow dish, combine the breadcrumbs and grated Parmesan cheese.

Dip each eggplant slice into the beaten eggs, then coat it in the breadcrumb mixture, pressing gently to adhere. Repeat with all eggplant slices.

Heat olive oil in a large skillet over medium-high heat. Fry the breaded eggplant slices in batches until golden brown and crispy on both sides, about 2-3 minutes per side. Add more oil as needed between batches. Transfer the fried eggplant slices to a paper towel-lined plate to drain excess oil.

Spread a thin layer of marinara sauce on the bottom of a baking dish. Arrange a single layer of fried eggplant slices on top of the sauce.

Spoon more marinara sauce over the eggplant slices, then sprinkle with shredded mozzarella cheese.

Repeat the layers of eggplant, sauce, and cheese until all the ingredients are used up, finishing with a layer of mozzarella cheese on top.

Cover the baking dish with aluminum foil and bake in the preheated oven for 25-30 minutes, or until the cheese is melted and bubbly.

Remove the foil from the baking dish and bake for an additional 5-10 minutes, or until the cheese is golden brown and slightly crispy.

Remove the Eggplant Parmesan from the oven and let it cool for a few minutes before serving.

Garnish with chopped fresh basil leaves, if desired.
Serve the Eggplant Parmesan hot as a delicious and satisfying main dish.

Enjoy your homemade Eggplant Parmesan! This classic Italian dish is perfect for a cozy family dinner or special occasion. Serve it with a side of pasta or a green salad for a complete meal.

Sheet Pan Lemon Herb Chicken with Roasted Vegetables

Ingredients:

For the chicken:

- 4 boneless, skinless chicken breasts
- 2 tablespoons olive oil
- 2 cloves garlic, minced
- Zest and juice of 1 lemon
- 1 tablespoon fresh thyme leaves (or 1 teaspoon dried thyme)
- 1 tablespoon fresh rosemary leaves (or 1 teaspoon dried rosemary)
- Salt and pepper, to taste

For the vegetables:

- 2 cups baby potatoes, halved
- 2 cups carrots, sliced into 1-inch pieces
- 2 cups broccoli florets
- 2 cups cherry tomatoes
- 2 tablespoons olive oil
- Salt and pepper, to taste
- 1 teaspoon Italian seasoning

Optional garnish:

- Fresh parsley, chopped
- Lemon slices

Instructions:

Preheat your oven to 400°F (200°C). Line a large baking sheet with parchment paper or aluminum foil for easy cleanup.

In a small bowl, whisk together the olive oil, minced garlic, lemon zest, lemon juice, thyme, rosemary, salt, and pepper to make the marinade for the chicken.

Place the chicken breasts in a resealable plastic bag or shallow dish, and pour the marinade over the chicken. Seal the bag or cover the dish, and marinate the chicken in the refrigerator for at least 30 minutes, or up to overnight for maximum flavor.

In a separate large bowl, toss the baby potatoes, carrots, broccoli florets, and cherry tomatoes with olive oil, salt, pepper, and Italian seasoning until evenly coated.

Spread the seasoned vegetables in a single layer on the prepared baking sheet.

Remove the chicken breasts from the marinade, allowing any excess marinade to drip off. Place the chicken on the baking sheet with the vegetables.

Bake in the preheated oven for 25-30 minutes, or until the chicken is cooked through and the vegetables are tender, flipping the chicken halfway through cooking.
Once the chicken is cooked through, remove the baking sheet from the oven and let it rest for a few minutes.
Garnish with chopped fresh parsley and lemon slices, if desired.
Serve the Sheet Pan Lemon Herb Chicken with Roasted Vegetables hot and enjoy!

This Sheet Pan Lemon Herb Chicken with Roasted Vegetables is a complete and satisfying meal that's easy to make and bursting with flavor. Feel free to customize the vegetables with your favorites, such as bell peppers, zucchini, or Brussels sprouts.

Tuna Salad Lettuce Wraps

Ingredients:

- 2 cans (5 oz each) tuna, drained
- 1/4 cup mayonnaise
- 1 tablespoon Dijon mustard
- 1 tablespoon lemon juice
- 1/4 cup finely diced celery
- 1/4 cup finely diced red onion
- Salt and pepper, to taste
- Lettuce leaves, for wrapping (such as romaine, butter lettuce, or iceberg)

Optional add-ins:

- Diced pickles or relish
- Chopped fresh herbs (such as parsley, dill, or chives)
- Sliced avocado
- Sliced cucumber
- Tomato slices

Instructions:

In a medium bowl, combine the drained tuna, mayonnaise, Dijon mustard, lemon juice, diced celery, and diced red onion. Mix until well combined.

Taste the tuna salad and season with salt and pepper to taste. Adjust the amount of mayonnaise, mustard, or lemon juice as needed to achieve your desired flavor and consistency.

Arrange the lettuce leaves on a serving platter or individual plates.

Spoon a generous amount of the tuna salad onto each lettuce leaf.

If desired, top the tuna salad with any optional add-ins such as diced pickles, chopped fresh herbs, sliced avocado, cucumber, or tomato.

Serve the Tuna Salad Lettuce Wraps immediately as a light and refreshing meal or snack.

Enjoy your delicious and nutritious Tuna Salad Lettuce Wraps!

These Tuna Salad Lettuce Wraps are perfect for a quick and easy lunch or light dinner. They're packed with protein, fiber, and healthy fats, making them a satisfying and nutritious option. Feel free to customize the tuna salad with your favorite ingredients and toppings to suit your taste preferences.

Cauliflower Crust Pizza

Ingredients:

For the cauliflower crust:

- 1 medium head cauliflower, cut into florets
- 1/4 cup grated Parmesan cheese
- 1/4 cup shredded mozzarella cheese
- 1/2 teaspoon dried oregano
- 1/2 teaspoon garlic powder
- 1/4 teaspoon salt
- 1/4 teaspoon black pepper
- 2 eggs, beaten

For the toppings:

- 1/2 cup pizza sauce or marinara sauce
- 1 cup shredded mozzarella cheese
- Your favorite pizza toppings (such as pepperoni, sliced bell peppers, onions, mushrooms, olives, etc.)

Instructions:

Preheat your oven to 425°F (220°C). Line a baking sheet or pizza stone with parchment paper.

Place the cauliflower florets in a food processor and pulse until they resemble fine crumbs, similar to rice.

Transfer the cauliflower crumbs to a microwave-safe bowl and microwave on high for 4-5 minutes, or until softened.

Allow the cauliflower to cool slightly, then transfer it to a clean kitchen towel or cheesecloth. Wrap the cauliflower in the towel and squeeze out as much moisture as possible. This step is crucial to ensure a crispy crust.

In a large mixing bowl, combine the squeezed cauliflower with grated Parmesan cheese, shredded mozzarella cheese, dried oregano, garlic powder, salt, black pepper, and beaten eggs. Mix until well combined.

Transfer the cauliflower mixture to the prepared baking sheet or pizza stone. Use your hands to spread it out into a thin, even layer, shaping it into a round pizza crust.

Bake the cauliflower crust in the preheated oven for 20-25 minutes, or until golden brown and crispy around the edges.

Once the crust is baked, remove it from the oven and spread pizza sauce evenly over the crust, leaving a small border around the edges.

Sprinkle shredded mozzarella cheese over the sauce, then add your favorite pizza toppings.

Return the pizza to the oven and bake for an additional 10-15 minutes, or until the cheese is melted and bubbly.

Remove the cauliflower crust pizza from the oven and let it cool for a few minutes before slicing.

Serve the Cauliflower Crust Pizza hot and enjoy!

This Cauliflower Crust Pizza is a delicious and low-carb alternative to traditional pizza crust. It's crispy, flavorful, and perfect for satisfying your pizza cravings while still keeping things light and healthy. Feel free to customize the toppings according to your preferences.

Chicken and Broccoli Casserole

Ingredients:

- 2 boneless, skinless chicken breasts, cooked and shredded
- 3 cups broccoli florets, steamed
- 2 cups cooked rice (white or brown)
- 1 can (10.5 oz) condensed cream of chicken soup
- 1/2 cup mayonnaise
- 1/2 cup sour cream
- 1 cup shredded cheddar cheese
- 1/4 cup grated Parmesan cheese
- 1 teaspoon garlic powder
- Salt and pepper, to taste
- 1 cup breadcrumbs
- 2 tablespoons butter, melted

Instructions:

Preheat your oven to 350°F (175°C). Grease a 9x13-inch baking dish with cooking spray or butter.

In a large mixing bowl, combine the shredded chicken, steamed broccoli florets, and cooked rice.

In a separate bowl, whisk together the condensed cream of chicken soup, mayonnaise, sour cream, shredded cheddar cheese, grated Parmesan cheese, garlic powder, salt, and pepper until well combined.

Pour the soup mixture over the chicken, broccoli, and rice mixture, and stir until everything is evenly coated.

Transfer the mixture to the prepared baking dish and spread it out into an even layer.

In a small bowl, combine the breadcrumbs and melted butter, and mix until the breadcrumbs are coated with butter.

Sprinkle the buttered breadcrumbs evenly over the top of the casserole.

Cover the baking dish with aluminum foil and bake in the preheated oven for 25 minutes.

Remove the foil and bake for an additional 10-15 minutes, or until the casserole is bubbly and the breadcrumbs are golden brown.

Remove the Chicken and Broccoli Casserole from the oven and let it cool for a few minutes before serving.

Serve the casserole hot and enjoy!

This Chicken and Broccoli Casserole is a comforting and hearty dish that's perfect for a cozy family dinner. It's creamy, cheesy, and packed with flavor, making it a surefire crowd-pleaser. Feel free to customize the casserole with your favorite ingredients or add extra seasonings for additional flavor.

Veggie-loaded Turkey Meatloaf

Ingredients:

- 1 lb (450g) ground turkey
- 1/2 cup grated zucchini
- 1/2 cup grated carrots
- 1/2 cup diced bell peppers (any color)
- 1/4 cup finely chopped onion
- 2 cloves garlic, minced
- 1/2 cup breadcrumbs
- 1/4 cup grated Parmesan cheese
- 1/4 cup ketchup
- 1 tablespoon Worcestershire sauce
- 1 teaspoon dried oregano
- 1 teaspoon dried thyme
- 1 teaspoon paprika
- Salt and pepper, to taste
- 1 egg, beaten

Instructions:

Preheat your oven to 375°F (190°C). Grease a loaf pan with cooking spray or olive oil.

In a large mixing bowl, combine the ground turkey, grated zucchini, grated carrots, diced bell peppers, chopped onion, minced garlic, breadcrumbs, grated Parmesan cheese, ketchup, Worcestershire sauce, dried oregano, dried thyme, paprika, salt, pepper, and beaten egg. Mix until all ingredients are well combined.

Transfer the turkey mixture to the prepared loaf pan and press it down evenly.

Spread a thin layer of ketchup over the top of the meatloaf for added flavor and moisture.

Bake in the preheated oven for 50-60 minutes, or until the meatloaf is cooked through and the internal temperature reaches 165°F (75°C).

Remove the meatloaf from the oven and let it rest for a few minutes before slicing.

Slice the meatloaf and serve it hot, garnished with fresh herbs if desired.

Enjoy your veggie-loaded Turkey Meatloaf!

This Turkey Meatloaf is packed with nutritious veggies and flavorful seasonings, making it a healthier twist on the classic comfort food. Serve it with your favorite sides such as mashed potatoes, roasted vegetables, or a side salad for a complete and satisfying meal. leftovers make for great sandwiches the next day too!

Mexican Quinoa Stuffed Peppers

Ingredients:

- 4 large bell peppers (any color), halved and seeds removed
- 1 cup quinoa, rinsed
- 2 cups vegetable broth or water
- 1 tablespoon olive oil
- 1 small onion, diced
- 2 cloves garlic, minced
- 1 bell pepper (any color), diced
- 1 can (15 oz) black beans, drained and rinsed
- 1 can (15 oz) diced tomatoes, drained
- 1 cup corn kernels (fresh, frozen, or canned)
- 1 teaspoon ground cumin
- 1 teaspoon chili powder
- Salt and pepper, to taste
- 1 cup shredded cheese (cheddar, Monterey Jack, or Mexican blend)
- Fresh cilantro, chopped, for garnish (optional)
- Avocado slices, for serving (optional)
- Lime wedges, for serving (optional)

Instructions:

Preheat your oven to 375°F (190°C). Grease a baking dish large enough to fit the halved bell peppers.

In a medium saucepan, bring the vegetable broth or water to a boil. Add the quinoa, reduce the heat to low, cover, and simmer for 15-20 minutes, or until the quinoa is cooked and the liquid is absorbed.

While the quinoa is cooking, heat olive oil in a large skillet over medium heat. Add the diced onion and minced garlic, and cook until softened and fragrant, about 3-4 minutes.

Add the diced bell pepper to the skillet and cook for another 2-3 minutes.

Stir in the black beans, diced tomatoes, corn kernels, ground cumin, chili powder, salt, and pepper. Cook for 3-4 minutes, until heated through and well combined.

Once the quinoa is cooked, add it to the skillet with the bean and vegetable mixture. Stir until everything is evenly combined.

Arrange the halved bell peppers in the greased baking dish, cut side up.

Spoon the quinoa and bean mixture into each bell pepper half, pressing down gently to pack it in.

Sprinkle shredded cheese over the top of each stuffed pepper.

Cover the baking dish with aluminum foil and bake in the preheated oven for 25-30 minutes, or until the peppers are tender and the cheese is melted and bubbly.

Remove the foil from the baking dish and bake for an additional 5 minutes, or until the cheese is golden brown.
Remove the Mexican Quinoa Stuffed Peppers from the oven and let them cool for a few minutes before serving.
Garnish with chopped fresh cilantro, avocado slices, and lime wedges, if desired.
Serve the stuffed peppers hot and enjoy!

These Mexican Quinoa Stuffed Peppers are flavorful, nutritious, and packed with protein and fiber. They make for a satisfying vegetarian meal that's perfect for lunch or dinner. Feel free to customize the filling with your favorite ingredients and adjust the seasonings to your taste preferences.

Greek Salad with Grilled Chicken

Ingredients:

For the grilled chicken:

- 2 boneless, skinless chicken breasts
- 2 tablespoons olive oil
- 1 tablespoon lemon juice
- 2 cloves garlic, minced
- 1 teaspoon dried oregano
- Salt and pepper, to taste

For the salad:

- 4 cups mixed salad greens (such as lettuce, spinach, or arugula)
- 1 cucumber, diced
- 1 cup cherry tomatoes, halved
- 1/2 red onion, thinly sliced
- 1/2 cup Kalamata olives, pitted
- 1/2 cup crumbled feta cheese
- 2 tablespoons chopped fresh parsley

For the dressing:

- 1/4 cup extra virgin olive oil
- 2 tablespoons red wine vinegar
- 1 teaspoon Dijon mustard
- 1 clove garlic, minced
- 1/2 teaspoon dried oregano
- Salt and pepper, to taste

Instructions:

In a small bowl, whisk together the olive oil, lemon juice, minced garlic, dried oregano, salt, and pepper to make the marinade for the grilled chicken. Place the chicken breasts in a resealable plastic bag or shallow dish, and pour the marinade over the chicken. Seal the bag or cover the dish, and marinate the chicken in the refrigerator for at least 30 minutes, or up to overnight for maximum flavor.

Preheat your grill or grill pan over medium-high heat. Remove the chicken from the marinade and discard the excess marinade. Grill the chicken breasts for 6-8 minutes per side, or until cooked through and no longer pink in the center.

Remove from the grill and let them rest for a few minutes before slicing.

In a large salad bowl, combine the mixed salad greens, diced cucumber, halved cherry tomatoes, thinly sliced red onion, Kalamata olives, crumbled feta cheese, and chopped fresh parsley.

In a small jar or bowl, combine the extra virgin olive oil, red wine vinegar, Dijon mustard, minced garlic, dried oregano, salt, and pepper. Shake or whisk until well combined to make the dressing.

Drizzle the dressing over the salad and toss until everything is evenly coated.

Divide the salad among serving plates or bowls.

Slice the grilled chicken breasts and arrange them on top of the salad.

Serve the Greek Salad with Grilled Chicken immediately and enjoy!

This Greek Salad with Grilled Chicken is light, refreshing, and bursting with Mediterranean flavors. It's perfect for a healthy and satisfying lunch or dinner. Feel free to customize the salad with your favorite ingredients and adjust the dressing to your taste preferences.

Broccoli Cheddar Soup

Ingredients:

- 4 cups broccoli florets (about 2 medium heads)
- 3 tablespoons unsalted butter
- 1 small onion, diced
- 2 cloves garlic, minced
- 1/4 cup all-purpose flour
- 4 cups low-sodium chicken or vegetable broth
- 1 cup whole milk
- 1 cup heavy cream
- 2 cups shredded sharp cheddar cheese
- Salt and pepper, to taste

Instructions:

In a large pot or Dutch oven, melt the butter over medium heat.

Add the diced onion and minced garlic to the pot and cook, stirring occasionally, until softened, about 3-4 minutes.

Sprinkle the flour over the onions and garlic, and cook, stirring constantly, for 1-2 minutes to make a roux.

Slowly whisk in the chicken or vegetable broth until smooth. Bring the mixture to a simmer.

Add the broccoli florets to the pot and simmer until tender, about 8-10 minutes.

Use an immersion blender to blend the soup until smooth, or transfer the soup to a blender and blend in batches until smooth. (Be careful when blending hot liquids.)

Return the blended soup to the pot (if necessary) and stir in the milk and heavy cream.

Bring the soup back to a simmer, then reduce the heat to low.

Gradually stir in the shredded cheddar cheese until melted and smooth.

Season the soup with salt and pepper, to taste.

Continue to simmer the soup for an additional 5-10 minutes to allow the flavors to meld together.

Serve the Broccoli Cheddar Soup hot, garnished with extra shredded cheddar cheese, if desired.

Enjoy your delicious and creamy Broccoli Cheddar Soup!

This Broccoli Cheddar Soup is creamy, cheesy, and packed with flavor. It's perfect for a comforting meal on a chilly day. Serve it with crusty bread or a side salad for a complete and satisfying meal.

Veggie and Bean Burrito Bowls

Ingredients:

For the burrito bowls:

- 1 cup quinoa, rinsed
- 2 cups vegetable broth or water
- 1 tablespoon olive oil
- 1 small onion, diced
- 2 cloves garlic, minced
- 1 bell pepper, diced
- 1 zucchini, diced
- 1 cup corn kernels (fresh, frozen, or canned)
- 1 can (15 oz) black beans, drained and rinsed
- 1 teaspoon ground cumin
- 1 teaspoon chili powder
- Salt and pepper, to taste

For serving:

- Sliced avocado
- Chopped fresh cilantro
- Lime wedges
- Salsa or pico de gallo
- Sour cream or Greek yogurt (optional)
- Shredded cheese (optional)

Instructions:

In a medium saucepan, bring the vegetable broth or water to a boil. Add the quinoa, reduce the heat to low, cover, and simmer for 15-20 minutes, or until the quinoa is cooked and the liquid is absorbed.

While the quinoa is cooking, heat olive oil in a large skillet over medium heat. Add the diced onion and cook until softened, about 3-4 minutes.

Add the minced garlic, diced bell pepper, and diced zucchini to the skillet. Cook for another 3-4 minutes, until the vegetables are tender.

Stir in the corn kernels, black beans, ground cumin, chili powder, salt, and pepper. Cook for an additional 2-3 minutes, until heated through and well combined.

Once the quinoa is cooked, fluff it with a fork and divide it among serving bowls.

Top each bowl of quinoa with the cooked veggie and bean mixture.

Garnish the burrito bowls with sliced avocado, chopped fresh cilantro, and lime wedges.

Serve the Veggie and Bean Burrito Bowls with salsa or pico de gallo, sour cream or Greek yogurt (if using), and shredded cheese (if using).
Enjoy your delicious and nutritious burrito bowls!

These Veggie and Bean Burrito Bowls are packed with protein, fiber, and flavor, making them a satisfying and wholesome meal. Feel free to customize the bowls with your favorite toppings and adjust the seasonings to your taste preferences. They're perfect for a quick and easy weeknight dinner or meal prep for lunches throughout the week.

Baked Salmon with Asparagus

Ingredients:

- 4 salmon fillets (about 6 ounces each), skin-on or skinless
- 1 bunch asparagus, tough ends trimmed
- 2 tablespoons olive oil
- 2 cloves garlic, minced
- 1 lemon, thinly sliced
- Salt and pepper, to taste
- Fresh dill or parsley, chopped, for garnish (optional)
  Preheat your oven to 400°F (200°C). Line a baking sheet with parchment paper or aluminum foil for easy cleanup.
  Arrange the salmon fillets and asparagus on the prepared baking sheet. Drizzle the olive oil over the salmon and asparagus.
  Rub the minced garlic evenly over the salmon fillets, then season them with salt and pepper to taste.
  Place lemon slices on top of each salmon fillet.
  Bake in the preheated oven for 12-15 minutes, or until the salmon is cooked through and flakes easily with a fork. The cooking time may vary depending on the thickness of your salmon fillets, so adjust accordingly.
  While the salmon is baking, the asparagus will also roast and become tender.
  Once the salmon is cooked, remove the baking sheet from the oven.
  Serve the Baked Salmon with Asparagus hot, garnished with chopped fresh dill or parsley, if desired.
  Enjoy your delicious and nutritious meal!

This Baked Salmon with Asparagus is a simple and healthy dish that's perfect for a quick weeknight dinner or a special occasion. The salmon is tender and flavorful, and the roasted asparagus adds a lovely touch of freshness. Feel free to customize the dish with your favorite herbs and seasonings, and serve it with a side of rice or quinoa for a complete meal.

Beef and Cabbage Stir-Fry

Ingredients:

- 1 lb (450g) beef sirloin or flank steak, thinly sliced against the grain
- 3 cups cabbage, thinly sliced
- 1 bell pepper, thinly sliced
- 1 onion, thinly sliced
- 3 cloves garlic, minced
- 2 tablespoons soy sauce
- 1 tablespoon oyster sauce
- 1 tablespoon hoisin sauce
- 1 tablespoon sesame oil
- 1 teaspoon cornstarch
- 1 teaspoon sugar
- 2 tablespoons vegetable oil, for cooking
- Salt and pepper, to taste
- Cooked rice, for serving
- Chopped green onions and sesame seeds, for garnish (optional)

Instructions:

In a small bowl, whisk together the soy sauce, oyster sauce, hoisin sauce, sesame oil, cornstarch, and sugar to make the sauce. Set aside.

Heat 1 tablespoon of vegetable oil in a large skillet or wok over medium-high heat.

Add the thinly sliced beef to the skillet in a single layer. Cook for 1-2 minutes per side, or until browned and cooked through. Remove the beef from the skillet and set aside.

In the same skillet, add the remaining tablespoon of vegetable oil. Add the sliced onion and bell pepper to the skillet. Stir-fry for 2-3 minutes, or until the vegetables are slightly softened.

Add the minced garlic to the skillet and cook for an additional 1 minute, until fragrant.

Add the thinly sliced cabbage to the skillet. Stir-fry for 3-4 minutes, or until the cabbage is wilted and tender.

Return the cooked beef to the skillet. Pour the sauce over the beef and vegetables in the skillet. Stir well to coat everything evenly with the sauce.

Cook for an additional 2-3 minutes, or until the sauce has thickened slightly and everything is heated through.

Season the Beef and Cabbage Stir-Fry with salt and pepper, to taste.
Serve the stir-fry hot over cooked rice.
Garnish with chopped green onions and sesame seeds, if desired.
Enjoy your delicious Beef and Cabbage Stir-Fry!

This Beef and Cabbage Stir-Fry is flavorful, hearty, and perfect for a quick and easy weeknight dinner. It's loaded with tender beef, crunchy vegetables, and a savory sauce that's sure to satisfy your cravings. Feel free to customize the stir-fry with your favorite vegetables or add some heat with a sprinkle of red pepper flakes.

Spinach and Feta Turkey Burgers

Ingredients:

- 1 lb (450g) ground turkey
- 1 cup fresh spinach, finely chopped
- 1/2 cup crumbled feta cheese
- 2 cloves garlic, minced
- 1/4 cup breadcrumbs
- 1 egg, beaten
- 1 tablespoon olive oil
- Salt and pepper, to taste
- Hamburger buns, for serving
- Lettuce, tomato, onion, and other burger toppings, as desired

Instructions:

In a large mixing bowl, combine the ground turkey, chopped spinach, crumbled feta cheese, minced garlic, breadcrumbs, beaten egg, olive oil, salt, and pepper. Mix until all ingredients are well combined.

Divide the turkey mixture into equal portions and shape them into burger patties.

Heat a grill pan or skillet over medium-high heat. Lightly grease the pan with olive oil or cooking spray.

Place the turkey burgers on the grill pan or skillet and cook for 5-6 minutes on each side, or until cooked through and nicely browned on the outside. Make sure the internal temperature of the burgers reaches 165°F (75°C).

While the burgers are cooking, lightly toast the hamburger buns if desired.

Once the turkey burgers are cooked, remove them from the heat and let them rest for a few minutes.

Assemble the burgers by placing each turkey patty on a hamburger bun. Add your desired toppings such as lettuce, tomato, onion, avocado, or any other condiments you prefer.

Serve the Spinach and Feta Turkey Burgers hot and enjoy!

These Spinach and Feta Turkey Burgers are flavorful, juicy, and packed with protein. The combination of spinach and feta adds a delicious Mediterranean twist to classic turkey burgers. Serve them with your favorite burger fixings for a satisfying meal that's perfect for lunch or dinner.

BBQ Chicken Stuffed Sweet Potatoes

Ingredients:

- 4 medium sweet potatoes
- 2 cups cooked shredded chicken (rotisserie chicken works well)
- 1/2 cup barbecue sauce (use your favorite)
- 1/4 cup diced red onion
- 1/4 cup diced bell pepper (any color)
- 1/4 cup shredded cheddar cheese
- 2 tablespoons chopped fresh cilantro (optional)
- Salt and pepper, to taste

Instructions:

Preheat your oven to 400°F (200°C).

Scrub the sweet potatoes clean and pierce them several times with a fork. Place them on a baking sheet lined with parchment paper.

Bake the sweet potatoes in the preheated oven for 45-60 minutes, or until they are tender and easily pierced with a fork.

While the sweet potatoes are baking, prepare the BBQ chicken filling. In a large mixing bowl, combine the shredded chicken, barbecue sauce, diced red onion, and diced bell pepper. Mix until everything is well coated.

Once the sweet potatoes are cooked, remove them from the oven and let them cool slightly.

Carefully slice each sweet potato lengthwise down the center, without cutting all the way through.

Gently fluff the insides of the sweet potatoes with a fork.

Divide the BBQ chicken mixture evenly among the sweet potatoes, spooning it into the center of each one.

Sprinkle shredded cheddar cheese over the top of each stuffed sweet potato.

Return the stuffed sweet potatoes to the oven and bake for an additional 5-10 minutes, or until the cheese is melted and bubbly.

Remove the stuffed sweet potatoes from the oven and sprinkle chopped fresh cilantro over the top, if desired.

Season with salt and pepper to taste.

Serve the BBQ Chicken Stuffed Sweet Potatoes hot and enjoy!

These BBQ Chicken Stuffed Sweet Potatoes are a delicious and satisfying meal that's perfect for

busy weeknights. They're loaded with flavor and packed with protein, fiber, and nutrients. Feel free to customize the toppings and add your favorite ingredients such as avocado, diced tomatoes, or sour cream.

Chickpea Curry

Ingredients:

- 2 tablespoons oil (such as vegetable or coconut oil)
- 1 onion, finely chopped
- 3 cloves garlic, minced
- 1 tablespoon grated ginger
- 1 tablespoon curry powder
- 1 teaspoon ground cumin
- 1 teaspoon ground coriander
- 1/2 teaspoon turmeric powder
- 1/4 teaspoon cayenne pepper (optional, for heat)
- 1 can (15 oz) chickpeas, drained and rinsed
- 1 can (14 oz) diced tomatoes
- 1 can (13.5 oz) coconut milk
- 1 cup vegetable broth
- 2 cups spinach leaves (or kale), chopped
- Salt and pepper, to taste
- Cooked rice, for serving
- Chopped fresh cilantro, for garnish
- Lime wedges, for serving

Instructions:

Heat the oil in a large skillet or pot over medium heat. Add the chopped onion and cook until softened, about 5 minutes.

Add the minced garlic and grated ginger to the skillet, and cook for another 1-2 minutes, until fragrant.

Stir in the curry powder, ground cumin, ground coriander, turmeric powder, and cayenne pepper (if using). Cook for 1 minute, stirring constantly, until the spices are toasted and fragrant.

Add the drained and rinsed chickpeas to the skillet, along with the diced tomatoes (with their juices), coconut milk, and vegetable broth. Stir to combine.

Bring the mixture to a simmer, then reduce the heat to low. Cover and let it simmer gently for about 15-20 minutes, stirring occasionally, until the flavors have melded together and the sauce has thickened slightly.

Stir in the chopped spinach leaves (or kale) and let them wilt into the curry. Cook for an additional 2-3 minutes.

Taste and adjust the seasoning with salt and pepper, if needed.

Serve the Chickpea Curry hot over cooked rice.

Garnish with chopped fresh cilantro and serve with lime wedges on the side for squeezing over the curry.

Enjoy your delicious and flavorful Chickpea Curry!

This Chickpea Curry is hearty, flavorful, and packed with protein and fiber. It's perfect for a quick and satisfying weeknight meal, and leftovers taste even better the next day. Feel free to customize the curry with your favorite vegetables or add extra spices for more heat.

Shrimp and Vegetable Skewers

Ingredients:

- 1 lb (450g) large shrimp, peeled and deveined
- 1 zucchini, sliced into rounds
- 1 bell pepper (any color), cut into chunks
- 1 red onion, cut into chunks
- 8-10 cherry tomatoes
- Wooden skewers, soaked in water for 30 minutes to prevent burning
- 2 tablespoons olive oil
- 2 cloves garlic, minced
- 1 teaspoon dried oregano
- 1 teaspoon paprika
- Salt and pepper, to taste
- Lemon wedges, for serving
- Chopped fresh parsley or cilantro, for garnish (optional)

Instructions:

Preheat your grill or grill pan to medium-high heat.

In a small bowl, whisk together the olive oil, minced garlic, dried oregano, paprika, salt, and pepper to make the marinade.

Thread the shrimp, zucchini slices, bell pepper chunks, red onion chunks, and cherry tomatoes onto the soaked wooden skewers, alternating between the ingredients.

Place the assembled skewers on a baking sheet or tray, and brush them with the prepared marinade, coating them evenly on all sides.

Once the grill is hot, place the skewers on the grill grate. Cook for 2-3 minutes on each side, or until the shrimp is pink and opaque and the vegetables are tender and slightly charred.

Remove the skewers from the grill and transfer them to a serving platter.

Garnish the Shrimp and Vegetable Skewers with chopped fresh parsley or cilantro, if desired.

Serve hot with lemon wedges on the side for squeezing over the skewers.

Enjoy your flavorful and colorful Shrimp and Vegetable Skewers!

These Shrimp and Vegetable Skewers are perfect for summer grilling or any time you want a quick and healthy meal. They're packed with flavor, protein, and nutrients, and they're easy to customize with your favorite vegetables and seasonings. Serve them as a main dish or as part of a barbecue spread with your favorite sides and sauces.

Pesto Zoodles with Grilled Chicken

Ingredients:

For the Pesto:

- 2 cups fresh basil leaves, packed
- 1/2 cup grated Parmesan cheese
- 1/4 cup pine nuts or walnuts
- 2 cloves garlic, minced
- 1/4 cup olive oil
- Salt and pepper, to taste

For the Zoodles:

- 4 medium zucchini
- 2 tablespoons olive oil
- Salt and pepper, to taste

For the Grilled Chicken:

- 2 boneless, skinless chicken breasts
- Salt and pepper, to taste
- 1 tablespoon olive oil
- 1 teaspoon Italian seasoning (optional)

Instructions:

For the Pesto:

In a food processor or blender, combine the basil leaves, grated Parmesan cheese, pine nuts or walnuts, and minced garlic.
Pulse until finely chopped.
With the food processor or blender running, slowly drizzle in the olive oil until the pesto reaches your desired consistency.
Season with salt and pepper, to taste. Set aside.

For the Zoodles:

Using a spiralizer, spiralize the zucchini into noodles. If you don't have a spiralizer, you can use a julienne peeler or vegetable peeler to make long, thin strips.
Heat 2 tablespoons of olive oil in a large skillet over medium heat.
Add the zucchini noodles to the skillet and sauté for 2-3 minutes, or until just tender.
Season with salt and pepper, to taste.

For the Grilled Chicken:

Preheat your grill or grill pan to medium-high heat.
Season the chicken breasts with salt, pepper, and Italian seasoning (if using).
Drizzle the chicken breasts with olive oil.
Grill the chicken breasts for 6-7 minutes on each side, or until cooked through and no longer pink in the center.
Remove the chicken breasts from the grill and let them rest for a few minutes before slicing.

Assembly:

Divide the cooked zoodles among serving plates.
Top the zoodles with a spoonful of pesto.
Slice the grilled chicken breasts and arrange them over the pesto zoodles.
Drizzle any remaining pesto over the grilled chicken.
Serve hot and enjoy!

This Pesto Zoodles with Grilled Chicken is a light and flavorful dish that's perfect for a quick and healthy meal. The fresh basil pesto adds a burst of herbaceous flavor, while the grilled chicken adds protein and substance. It's a great way to enjoy a satisfying meal while keeping things light and nutritious.

Turkey and Black Bean Chili

Ingredients:

- 1 tablespoon olive oil
- 1 onion, chopped
- 3 cloves garlic, minced
- 1 lb (450g) ground turkey
- 1 bell pepper, diced
- 1 jalapeño pepper, seeded and diced (optional, for heat)
- 1 can (15 oz) black beans, drained and rinsed
- 1 can (14.5 oz) diced tomatoes
- 2 cups chicken broth
- 2 tablespoons tomato paste
- 2 teaspoons chili powder
- 1 teaspoon ground cumin
- 1 teaspoon smoked paprika
- Salt and pepper, to taste
- Chopped fresh cilantro, for garnish
- Shredded cheddar cheese, for garnish (optional)
- Sour cream, for garnish (optional)
- Sliced green onions, for garnish (optional)
- Tortilla chips or cornbread, for serving

Instructions:

Heat the olive oil in a large pot or Dutch oven over medium heat. Add the chopped onion and cook until softened, about 5 minutes.

Add the minced garlic to the pot and cook for an additional 1-2 minutes, until fragrant.

Add the ground turkey to the pot, breaking it up with a spoon. Cook until browned and cooked through, about 6-8 minutes.

Stir in the diced bell pepper and jalapeño pepper (if using), and cook for another 2-3 minutes.

Add the drained and rinsed black beans, diced tomatoes (with their juices), chicken broth, tomato paste, chili powder, ground cumin, smoked paprika, salt, and pepper to the pot. Stir well to combine.

Bring the chili to a simmer, then reduce the heat to low. Cover and let it simmer gently for about 20-25 minutes, stirring occasionally, to allow the flavors to meld together and the chili to thicken slightly.

Taste and adjust the seasoning with salt and pepper, if needed.

Serve the Turkey and Black Bean Chili hot, garnished with chopped fresh cilantro, shredded cheddar cheese, sour cream, and sliced green onions, if desired.

Serve with tortilla chips or cornbread on the side for dipping or scooping.

Enjoy your delicious and hearty Turkey and Black Bean Chili!

This Turkey and Black Bean Chili is hearty, flavorful, and perfect for a cozy meal on a chilly day. It's packed with protein, fiber, and nutritious ingredients, making it a satisfying and wholesome dish. Feel free to customize the chili with your favorite toppings and adjust the seasonings to your taste preferences.

Caprese Salad with Balsamic Glaze

Ingredients:

- 3-4 ripe tomatoes, sliced
- 1 ball fresh mozzarella cheese, sliced
- Fresh basil leaves
- Salt and pepper, to taste
- Balsamic glaze (store-bought or homemade)

Instructions:

Arrange the sliced tomatoes and mozzarella cheese alternately on a serving platter or individual plates.
Tuck fresh basil leaves between the tomato and mozzarella slices.
Season the salad with salt and pepper, to taste.
Drizzle balsamic glaze over the salad just before serving. You can use store-bought balsamic glaze or make your own by simmering balsamic vinegar over low heat until it thickens and becomes syrupy.
Serve the Caprese Salad immediately as a refreshing appetizer or side dish.
Enjoy the delicious combination of flavors!

This Caprese Salad with Balsamic Glaze is simple to prepare but bursting with freshness and flavor. It's perfect for summer gatherings, picnics, or as a light and healthy starter for any meal.

Feel free to adjust the ingredients and quantities based on your preferences and the number of servings you need.

Veggie Stir-Fry with Tofu

Ingredients:

- 1 block firm tofu, drained and pressed
- 2 tablespoons soy sauce
- 1 tablespoon rice vinegar
- 1 tablespoon sesame oil
- 1 tablespoon cornstarch
- 2 tablespoons vegetable oil
- 2 cloves garlic, minced
- 1 tablespoon ginger, minced
- 1 bell pepper, sliced
- 1 carrot, julienned
- 1 cup broccoli florets
- 1 cup snow peas
- 1 cup sliced mushrooms
- Salt and pepper, to taste
- Cooked rice or noodles, for serving
- Sesame seeds and chopped green onions, for garnish (optional)

Instructions:

Cut the pressed tofu into cubes and place them in a bowl. In a separate small bowl, whisk together the soy sauce, rice vinegar, sesame oil, and cornstarch. Pour the marinade over the tofu cubes and gently toss to coat. Let the tofu marinate for at least 15 minutes.

Heat 1 tablespoon of vegetable oil in a large skillet or wok over medium-high heat. Add the marinated tofu cubes to the skillet in a single layer and cook for 3-4 minutes per side, or until golden brown and crispy. Remove the tofu from the skillet and set aside.

In the same skillet, add the remaining tablespoon of vegetable oil. Add the minced garlic and ginger, and sauté for 1 minute, until fragrant.

Add the sliced bell pepper, julienned carrot, broccoli florets, snow peas, and sliced mushrooms to the skillet. Stir-fry for 5-6 minutes, or until the vegetables are tender-crisp.

Return the cooked tofu to the skillet and toss everything together until heated through.

Season the stir-fry with salt and pepper, to taste.

Serve the Veggie Stir-Fry with Tofu hot over cooked rice or noodles.

Garnish with sesame seeds and chopped green onions, if desired.

Enjoy your delicious and nutritious Veggie Stir-Fry with Tofu!

This Veggie Stir-Fry with Tofu is packed with flavor and loaded with colorful vegetables and protein-rich tofu. It's a quick and easy meal that's perfect for busy weeknights. Feel free to customize the stir-fry with your favorite veggies and adjust the seasonings to your taste preferences.

Lentil Sloppy Joes

Ingredients:

- 1 cup dried green or brown lentils
- 2 cups vegetable broth or water
- 1 tablespoon olive oil
- 1 onion, finely chopped
- 2 cloves garlic, minced
- 1 bell pepper, diced
- 1 carrot, diced
- 1 celery stalk, diced
- 1 can (14.5 oz) diced tomatoes
- 2 tablespoons tomato paste
- 2 tablespoons maple syrup or brown sugar
- 2 tablespoons Worcestershire sauce (make sure it's vegetarian/vegan if needed)
- 1 tablespoon Dijon mustard
- 1 teaspoon chili powder
- 1/2 teaspoon smoked paprika
- Salt and pepper, to taste
- Hamburger buns or sandwich rolls, for serving

Instructions:

Rinse the lentils under cold water and drain.

In a medium saucepan, combine the lentils and vegetable broth or water. Bring to a boil, then reduce the heat to low, cover, and simmer for 20-25 minutes, or until the lentils are tender and most of the liquid is absorbed. Drain any excess liquid and set aside.

In a large skillet, heat the olive oil over medium heat. Add the chopped onion and cook until softened, about 5 minutes.

Add the minced garlic, diced bell pepper, diced carrot, and diced celery to the skillet. Cook for another 5 minutes, or until the vegetables are tender.

Stir in the cooked lentils, diced tomatoes (with their juices), tomato paste, maple syrup or brown sugar, Worcestershire sauce, Dijon mustard, chili powder, smoked paprika, salt, and pepper. Mix well to combine.

Bring the mixture to a simmer and cook for 10-15 minutes, stirring occasionally, until the flavors are blended and the mixture has thickened to your desired consistency.

Taste and adjust the seasoning, adding more salt, pepper, or spices as needed.

Serve the Lentil Sloppy Joes hot on hamburger buns or sandwich rolls.

Enjoy your delicious and hearty Lentil Sloppy Joes!

These Lentil Sloppy Joes are a vegetarian twist on the classic comfort food dish. They're packed with protein and fiber from the lentils and bursting with flavor from the savory and tangy sauce. Serve them with your favorite sides like coleslaw, potato chips, or pickles for a satisfying meal.

Greek Chicken Souvlaki with Tzatziki Sauce

Ingredients:

For the Chicken Souvlaki:

- 1.5 lbs (680g) boneless, skinless chicken breasts, cut into cubes
- 1/4 cup olive oil
- 3 cloves garlic, minced
- 1 tablespoon dried oregano
- 1 teaspoon dried thyme
- 1 teaspoon paprika
- 1/2 teaspoon ground cumin
- Juice of 1 lemon
- Salt and pepper, to taste
- Wooden skewers, soaked in water for 30 minutes

For the Tzatziki Sauce:

- 1 cup Greek yogurt
- 1/2 cucumber, grated and squeezed to remove excess moisture
- 2 cloves garlic, minced
- 1 tablespoon fresh lemon juice
- 1 tablespoon extra virgin olive oil
- 1 tablespoon chopped fresh dill (or 1 teaspoon dried dill)
- Salt and pepper, to taste

For Serving:

- Pita bread or flatbread
- Sliced tomatoes
- Sliced red onions
- Chopped fresh parsley or cilantro, for garnish

Instructions:

For the Chicken Souvlaki:

In a large bowl, combine the olive oil, minced garlic, dried oregano, dried thyme, paprika, ground cumin, lemon juice, salt, and pepper. Mix well to make the marinade.

Add the cubed chicken breasts to the marinade and toss until evenly coated.
Cover and refrigerate for at least 30 minutes, or up to 4 hours, to allow the flavors to meld.
Preheat your grill or grill pan over medium-high heat.
Thread the marinated chicken cubes onto the soaked wooden skewers.
Grill the chicken skewers for 6-8 minutes per side, or until the chicken is cooked through and has nice grill marks.

For the Tzatziki Sauce:

In a medium bowl, combine the Greek yogurt, grated cucumber, minced garlic, lemon juice, olive oil, chopped fresh dill, salt, and pepper. Mix well to combine.
Taste and adjust the seasoning, adding more salt, pepper, or lemon juice if needed.
Cover and refrigerate the tzatziki sauce until ready to serve.

To Serve:

Warm the pita bread or flatbread on the grill for a few seconds on each side.
Serve the grilled chicken souvlaki on warm pita bread or flatbread, topped with sliced tomatoes, sliced red onions, and a generous dollop of tzatziki sauce.
Garnish with chopped fresh parsley or cilantro.
Enjoy your delicious Greek Chicken Souvlaki with Tzatziki Sauce!

This Greek Chicken Souvlaki with Tzatziki Sauce is a flavorful and satisfying meal that's perfect for a summer barbecue or weeknight dinner. The tender and juicy chicken skewers paired with the creamy and tangy tzatziki sauce and fresh vegetables create a delicious combination of flavors and textures. Serve it with a side salad or Greek-style rice for a complete meal.

Cauliflower Fried Rice

Ingredients:

- 1 head of cauliflower
- 2 tablespoons oil (olive oil, sesame oil, or vegetable oil)
- 2 cloves garlic, minced
- 1 small onion, diced
- 1 cup mixed vegetables (such as carrots, peas, and bell peppers), diced
- 2 eggs, lightly beaten
- 2-3 tablespoons soy sauce or tamari (adjust to taste)
- Salt and pepper to taste
- Green onions, chopped (optional, for garnish)
- Sesame seeds (optional, for garnish)

Instructions:

Prepare the cauliflower rice by cutting the cauliflower into florets and pulsing them in a food processor until they resemble the texture of rice. Alternatively, you can grate the cauliflower using a box grater.

Heat 1 tablespoon of oil in a large skillet or wok over medium heat. Add the minced garlic and diced onion, and sauté until fragrant and translucent, about 2-3 minutes.

Add the mixed vegetables to the skillet and cook until they are tender, about 5-7 minutes.

Push the vegetables to one side of the skillet and add the beaten eggs to the empty side. Scramble the eggs until they are cooked through, then mix them with the vegetables.

Push the vegetable and egg mixture to the side again, and add the remaining tablespoon of oil to the empty side of the skillet. Add the cauliflower rice to the skillet and stir-fry for about 5-7 minutes, or until the cauliflower is tender but still slightly crisp.

Stir in the soy sauce or tamari, salt, and pepper, adjusting the seasoning to taste. Garnish with chopped green onions and sesame seeds if desired, then serve hot.

Feel free to customize this recipe by adding your favorite proteins such as cooked chicken, shrimp, or tofu, and additional seasonings like ginger or chili flakes for extra flavor. Enjoy your cauliflower fried rice as a delicious and nutritious alternative to traditional fried rice!

Buffalo Chicken Lettuce Wraps

Ingredients:

- 1 pound boneless, skinless chicken breasts, cooked and shredded
- 1/2 cup buffalo sauce (adjust to taste)
- 1/4 cup ranch or blue cheese dressing
- 1/4 cup diced celery
- 1/4 cup diced red onion
- 1/4 cup crumbled blue cheese (optional)
- Salt and pepper to taste
- Butter lettuce leaves (or any lettuce of your choice), washed and separated
- Optional toppings: diced tomatoes, avocado slices, chopped green onions

Instructions:

In a mixing bowl, combine the shredded chicken with the buffalo sauce, ranch or blue cheese dressing, diced celery, diced red onion, and crumbled blue cheese (if using). Mix until well combined.

Season the chicken mixture with salt and pepper to taste, adjusting the seasoning as needed.

Place a spoonful of the buffalo chicken mixture onto each lettuce leaf, spreading it out evenly.

Add any additional toppings you like, such as diced tomatoes, avocado slices, or chopped green onions.

Serve the buffalo chicken lettuce wraps immediately, and enjoy!

These lettuce wraps are perfect for a light lunch, dinner, or party appetizer. They're also easily customizable, so feel free to adjust the ingredients and toppings to suit your taste preferences. Enjoy the spicy kick of buffalo chicken without the guilt of fried wings!

Ratatouille

Ingredients:

- 1 large eggplant
- 2 medium zucchinis
- 1 large yellow onion
- 2 bell peppers (red, yellow, or orange)
- 4-5 ripe tomatoes
- 3 cloves garlic, minced
- 2-3 tablespoons olive oil
- 1 tablespoon tomato paste (optional)
- 1 teaspoon dried herbs de Provence (or a mixture of dried thyme, oregano, and basil)
- Salt and pepper to taste
- Fresh basil leaves, chopped, for garnish (optional)

Instructions:

Preheat your oven to 375°F (190°C).

Wash and prepare all the vegetables. Peel the eggplant if desired and cut it into 1-inch cubes. Slice the zucchinis into rounds. Peel and dice the onion. Core the bell peppers and slice them into strips. Dice the tomatoes or cut them into thick slices.

Heat 1 tablespoon of olive oil in a large skillet or Dutch oven over medium heat. Add the diced onion and minced garlic, and sauté until they are soft and translucent, about 5 minutes.

Add the eggplant cubes to the skillet and cook for another 5 minutes, stirring occasionally.

Push the vegetables to the side of the skillet and add another tablespoon of olive oil to the empty space. Add the sliced bell peppers and zucchini rounds, and cook for about 5 minutes until they start to soften.

Add the diced tomatoes (or tomato slices) to the skillet, along with the tomato paste (if using), dried herbs de Provence, salt, and pepper. Stir everything together gently.

Cover the skillet or Dutch oven with a lid and let the ratatouille simmer over low heat for about 20-30 minutes, stirring occasionally, until all the vegetables are tender and the flavors have melded together.

Taste and adjust the seasoning as needed, adding more salt, pepper, or herbs if desired.

Once cooked, you can serve the ratatouille hot, garnished with chopped fresh basil leaves if desired. It's traditionally served as a side dish or main course, often accompanied by crusty bread or rice.

Ratatouille can also be stored in the refrigerator for a few days and reheated for leftovers. It's a versatile dish that can be enjoyed on its own or served alongside grilled meats or fish. Enjoy this hearty and comforting French classic!

Black Bean and Corn Quesadillas

Ingredients:

- 1 can (15 oz) black beans, drained and rinsed
- 1 cup corn kernels (fresh, canned, or frozen)
- 1 cup shredded cheese (cheddar, Monterey Jack, or a blend)
- 1/2 cup diced bell peppers (any color)
- 1/4 cup chopped fresh cilantro (optional)
- 1 teaspoon ground cumin
- 1/2 teaspoon chili powder
- Salt and pepper to taste
- 4 large flour tortillas
- Cooking spray or olive oil, for cooking
- Salsa, sour cream, guacamole, or chopped tomatoes, for serving (optional)

Instructions:

In a mixing bowl, combine the black beans, corn kernels, shredded cheese, diced bell peppers, chopped cilantro (if using), ground cumin, and chili powder. Mix well to combine all the ingredients. Season with salt and pepper to taste.

Lay out one tortilla on a clean surface. Spread about 1/4 of the black bean and corn mixture evenly over one half of the tortilla, leaving a small border around the edges.

Fold the other half of the tortilla over the filling to create a half-moon shape. Repeat the process with the remaining tortillas and filling mixture.

Heat a large skillet or griddle over medium heat. Spray the surface lightly with cooking spray or brush with olive oil.

Carefully place the quesadillas in the skillet or griddle, cooking 2 at a time if necessary. Cook for 2-3 minutes on each side, or until the tortillas are golden brown and crispy, and the cheese is melted.

Remove the quesadillas from the skillet and let them cool for a minute before slicing them into wedges.

Serve the black bean and corn quesadillas hot, with your favorite toppings such as salsa, sour cream, guacamole, or chopped tomatoes on the side.

These quesadillas are versatile, so feel free to customize them with additional ingredients such as diced onions, jalapeños, or cooked chicken or beef. They're perfect for a quick lunch, dinner, or even as a party appetizer. Enjoy the delicious combination of flavors and textures in these tasty quesadillas!

Mediterranean Quinoa Salad

Ingredients:

- 1 cup quinoa, rinsed
- 2 cups water or vegetable broth
- 1 cup cherry tomatoes, halved
- 1 cucumber, diced
- 1/2 red onion, finely chopped
- 1/2 cup Kalamata olives, pitted and sliced
- 1/2 cup crumbled feta cheese
- 1/4 cup chopped fresh parsley
- 1/4 cup chopped fresh mint
- 1/4 cup extra virgin olive oil
- 2 tablespoons lemon juice
- 2 cloves garlic, minced
- 1 teaspoon dried oregano
- Salt and pepper to taste

Instructions:

In a medium saucepan, combine the quinoa and water or vegetable broth. Bring to a boil over medium-high heat, then reduce the heat to low, cover, and simmer for 15-20 minutes, or until the quinoa is cooked and the liquid is absorbed. Remove from heat and let it cool.

In a large mixing bowl, combine the cooked quinoa, cherry tomatoes, cucumber, red onion, Kalamata olives, crumbled feta cheese, chopped parsley, and chopped mint.

In a small bowl, whisk together the extra virgin olive oil, lemon juice, minced garlic, dried oregano, salt, and pepper to make the dressing.

Pour the dressing over the quinoa salad and toss gently to coat all the ingredients evenly.

Taste and adjust the seasoning as needed, adding more salt, pepper, or lemon juice if desired.

Cover the bowl and refrigerate the Mediterranean quinoa salad for at least 30 minutes to allow the flavors to meld together.

Before serving, give the salad a final toss and garnish with additional fresh herbs or crumbled feta cheese if desired.

This Mediterranean quinoa salad is perfect as a light and refreshing meal on its own, or as a side dish to accompany grilled chicken, fish, or lamb. It's also great for picnics, potlucks, or meal prep. Enjoy the burst of flavors and textures in every bite!

Sausage and Pepper Foil Packets

Ingredients:

- 4 Italian sausages (sweet or spicy), sliced into 1-inch pieces
- 2 bell peppers (any color), sliced
- 1 onion, sliced
- 2 cloves garlic, minced
- 2 tablespoons olive oil
- 1 teaspoon dried oregano
- 1 teaspoon dried basil
- Salt and pepper to taste
- Optional: crushed red pepper flakes for extra heat
- Fresh parsley or basil for garnish
- Cooked rice or crusty bread for serving

Instructions:

Preheat your grill to medium-high heat or preheat your oven to 425°F (220°C).
Cut four large pieces of heavy-duty aluminum foil, about 12x12 inches each.
In a large mixing bowl, combine the sliced Italian sausages, sliced bell peppers, sliced onion, minced garlic, olive oil, dried oregano, dried basil, salt, and pepper. Toss everything together until the sausages and vegetables are evenly coated with the seasonings.
Divide the sausage and pepper mixture evenly among the four pieces of foil, placing them in the center of each foil piece.
Fold the sides of the foil over the sausage and pepper mixture, then fold and crimp the edges to seal the packets securely.
Place the foil packets directly on the grill grates or on a baking sheet if using the oven.
Grill or bake the foil packets for about 15-20 minutes, or until the sausages are cooked through and the peppers and onions are tender. If grilling, flip the packets halfway through cooking.
Carefully open the foil packets (watch out for steam), and garnish the sausage and pepper mixture with fresh parsley or basil.
Serve the sausage and pepper foil packets hot, either on their own or over cooked rice or with crusty bread on the side.

These foil packets are convenient for outdoor cooking and cleanup, and they're packed with flavor from the sausage and peppers. Enjoy this simple and satisfying meal!

Tofu Vegetable Stir-Fry

Ingredients:

- 14 oz (400g) firm tofu, pressed and cubed
- 2 tablespoons soy sauce or tamari
- 1 tablespoon rice vinegar
- 1 tablespoon hoisin sauce
- 1 tablespoon sesame oil
- 1 tablespoon cornstarch
- 2 tablespoons vegetable oil, divided
- 2 cloves garlic, minced
- 1 tablespoon grated ginger
- 1 bell pepper, thinly sliced
- 1 medium carrot, julienned
- 1 cup broccoli florets
- 1 cup snap peas
- 1 cup sliced mushrooms
- Salt and pepper to taste
- Cooked rice or noodles, for serving

Instructions:

Press the tofu to remove excess moisture. Place the tofu between paper towels or clean kitchen towels and place a heavy object on top (like a cast-iron skillet). Let it press for at least 20-30 minutes.

In a small bowl, whisk together the soy sauce, rice vinegar, hoisin sauce, sesame oil, and cornstarch to make the sauce. Set aside.

Heat 1 tablespoon of vegetable oil in a large skillet or wok over medium-high heat. Add the cubed tofu and cook until golden brown on all sides, about 5-7 minutes. Remove the tofu from the skillet and set aside.

In the same skillet, add the remaining tablespoon of vegetable oil. Add the minced garlic and grated ginger, and sauté for about 1 minute until fragrant.

Add the sliced bell pepper, julienned carrot, broccoli florets, snap peas, and sliced mushrooms to the skillet. Stir-fry for 5-7 minutes, or until the vegetables are tender-crisp.

Return the cooked tofu to the skillet with the vegetables.

Pour the sauce over the tofu and vegetables, and stir well to coat everything evenly. Cook for another 2-3 minutes, or until the sauce has thickened slightly.
Taste and adjust the seasoning with salt and pepper if needed.
Serve the tofu vegetable stir-fry hot over cooked rice or noodles.

This tofu vegetable stir-fry is customizable, so feel free to add your favorite vegetables or adjust the seasonings according to your taste preferences. It's a healthy and flavorful dish that's sure to satisfy vegetarians and meat-eaters alike! Enjoy!

Spinach and Mushroom Quiche

Ingredients:

- 1 pie crust (store-bought or homemade)
- 1 tablespoon olive oil
- 8 oz (225g) mushrooms, sliced
- 2 cups fresh spinach leaves
- 1 small onion, finely chopped
- 2 cloves garlic, minced
- 4 large eggs
- 1 cup milk or half-and-half
- 1 cup shredded cheese (such as Swiss, Gruyere, or cheddar)
- Salt and pepper to taste
- Pinch of nutmeg (optional)
- Chopped fresh parsley or chives for garnish (optional)

Instructions:

Preheat your oven to 375°F (190°C).

Roll out the pie crust and press it into a 9-inch pie dish. Trim any excess crust hanging over the edges. If using a store-bought crust, follow the package instructions for pre-baking (also known as blind baking) the crust to prevent it from becoming soggy once the filling is added.

Heat the olive oil in a large skillet over medium heat. Add the sliced mushrooms and cook for 5-7 minutes, or until they are golden brown and any liquid released has evaporated.

Add the chopped onion and minced garlic to the skillet with the mushrooms, and cook for another 2-3 minutes until the onion is soft and translucent.

Add the fresh spinach leaves to the skillet and cook for 1-2 minutes, or until wilted. Remove the skillet from heat and let the mixture cool slightly.

In a mixing bowl, whisk together the eggs and milk (or half-and-half) until well combined. Season with salt, pepper, and a pinch of nutmeg if desired.

Spread the mushroom, spinach, and onion mixture evenly over the bottom of the pre-baked pie crust.

Sprinkle the shredded cheese over the top of the vegetable mixture.

Pour the egg mixture over the vegetables and cheese in the pie crust, ensuring that the filling is evenly distributed.

Place the quiche in the preheated oven and bake for 35-40 minutes, or until the center is set and the top is golden brown.
Remove the quiche from the oven and let it cool for a few minutes before slicing.
Garnish with chopped fresh parsley or chives if desired, then slice and serve.

This spinach and mushroom quiche is delicious served warm or at room temperature.

It's perfect for brunch gatherings, potlucks, or as a make-ahead meal for busy

weekdays. Enjoy the creamy, savory goodness of this classic dish!

Turkey and Veggie Skillet

Ingredients:

- 1 lb (450g) ground turkey
- 1 tablespoon olive oil
- 1 onion, diced
- 2 cloves garlic, minced
- 1 bell pepper, diced
- 1 zucchini, diced
- 1 cup cherry tomatoes, halved
- 1 teaspoon dried oregano
- 1 teaspoon dried basil
- Salt and pepper to taste
- Optional: red pepper flakes for heat
- Grated cheese for topping (such as Parmesan or mozzarella)
- Fresh parsley or basil for garnish

Instructions:

Heat olive oil in a large skillet over medium heat.
Add diced onion and minced garlic to the skillet, and sauté until softened and fragrant, about 2-3 minutes.
Add ground turkey to the skillet and cook, breaking it up with a spatula, until it's browned and cooked through.
Once the turkey is cooked, add diced bell pepper and zucchini to the skillet. Cook for another 3-4 minutes, or until the vegetables start to soften.
Stir in cherry tomatoes, dried oregano, dried basil, salt, pepper, and red pepper flakes (if using). Cook for an additional 2-3 minutes, or until the tomatoes begin to release their juices and the vegetables are cooked to your desired tenderness.
Taste and adjust seasoning if needed.
If desired, sprinkle grated cheese over the top of the skillet and let it melt slightly.
Remove the skillet from heat and garnish with fresh parsley or basil.
Serve the turkey and veggie skillet hot, either on its own or with a side of cooked rice, quinoa, or crusty bread.

This turkey and veggie skillet is versatile, so feel free to customize it with your favorite vegetables or spices. It's a healthy and flavorful meal that's perfect for busy weeknights. Enjoy!

Egg Roll in a Bowl

Ingredients:

- 1 lb (450g) ground pork or ground turkey
- 1 tablespoon sesame oil
- 1 onion, thinly sliced
- 3 cloves garlic, minced
- 1 tablespoon freshly grated ginger
- 1/4 cup soy sauce or tamari
- 1 tablespoon rice vinegar
- 1 tablespoon hoisin sauce (optional)
- 1 teaspoon sriracha or chili garlic sauce (adjust to taste)
- 1 head cabbage, thinly sliced
- 2 carrots, julienned or shredded
- 4 green onions, thinly sliced
- Salt and pepper to taste
- Sesame seeds for garnish (optional)
- Chopped fresh cilantro for garnish (optional)

Instructions:

Heat sesame oil in a large skillet or wok over medium-high heat.
Add ground pork or ground turkey to the skillet and cook, breaking it up with a spatula, until it's browned and cooked through.
Add sliced onion to the skillet and cook for 2-3 minutes, until it starts to soften.
Stir in minced garlic and freshly grated ginger, and cook for another 1-2 minutes until fragrant.
In a small bowl, whisk together soy sauce or tamari, rice vinegar, hoisin sauce (if using), and sriracha or chili garlic sauce.
Pour the sauce over the meat mixture in the skillet and stir to combine.
Add thinly sliced cabbage and julienned carrots to the skillet. Cook, stirring occasionally, for 5-7 minutes, or until the cabbage is wilted and the carrots are tender-crisp.
Stir in sliced green onions and season with salt and pepper to taste.
Remove the skillet from heat and garnish with sesame seeds and chopped fresh cilantro if desired.

Serve the egg roll in a bowl hot, garnished with additional green onions, sesame seeds, or cilantro if desired.

This egg roll in a bowl is a versatile dish that can be enjoyed on its own or served over cooked rice or cauliflower rice for a low-carb option. It's quick, easy, and packed with flavor, making it perfect for a satisfying weeknight dinner. Enjoy!

Veggie Packed Bolognese Sauce

Ingredients:

- 2 tablespoons olive oil
- 1 onion, finely chopped
- 2 carrots, finely chopped
- 2 celery stalks, finely chopped
- 1 bell pepper, finely chopped
- 2 cloves garlic, minced
- 1 zucchini, finely chopped
- 8 oz (225g) mushrooms, finely chopped
- 1 teaspoon dried oregano
- 1 teaspoon dried basil
- 1/2 teaspoon dried thyme
- 1/4 teaspoon red pepper flakes (optional, for heat)
- Salt and pepper to taste
- 1 can (28 oz) crushed tomatoes
- 1 can (6 oz) tomato paste
- 1 cup vegetable broth or water
- 1 tablespoon balsamic vinegar
- 2 bay leaves
- 1/4 cup chopped fresh parsley or basil
- Cooked pasta of your choice, for serving
- Grated Parmesan cheese, for serving (optional)

Instructions:

Heat olive oil in a large pot or Dutch oven over medium heat.
Add chopped onion, carrots, celery, and bell pepper to the pot. Cook, stirring occasionally, for about 5 minutes, or until the vegetables start to soften.
Add minced garlic, chopped zucchini, and chopped mushrooms to the pot. Cook for another 5 minutes, or until the vegetables are tender and any excess liquid from the mushrooms has evaporated.
Stir in dried oregano, dried basil, dried thyme, red pepper flakes (if using), salt, and pepper.
Add crushed tomatoes, tomato paste, vegetable broth or water, balsamic vinegar, and bay leaves to the pot. Stir to combine all the ingredients.

Bring the sauce to a simmer, then reduce the heat to low. Cover and let the sauce simmer for about 30 minutes to allow the flavors to meld together, stirring occasionally.

Taste the sauce and adjust the seasoning if needed, adding more salt, pepper, or herbs as desired.

Remove the bay leaves from the sauce and discard them.

Stir in chopped fresh parsley or basil.

Serve the veggie-packed Bolognese sauce hot over cooked pasta of your choice.

Optionally, garnish with grated Parmesan cheese before serving.

This veggie-packed Bolognese sauce is flavorful, hearty, and perfect for serving over pasta, spaghetti squash, or zucchini noodles for a low-carb option. Enjoy the wholesome goodness of this nutritious sauce!

Lemon Garlic Shrimp with Zucchini Noodles

Ingredients:

- 1 lb (450g) large shrimp, peeled and deveined
- 3-4 medium zucchini, spiralized into noodles
- 4 cloves garlic, minced
- 2 tablespoons olive oil
- Zest of 1 lemon
- Juice of 1 lemon
- 1/4 teaspoon red pepper flakes (optional, for heat)
- Salt and pepper to taste
- Chopped fresh parsley for garnish
- Grated Parmesan cheese for garnish (optional)

Instructions:

Pat the shrimp dry with paper towels and season them with salt and pepper.
Heat olive oil in a large skillet over medium heat. Add minced garlic and red pepper flakes (if using), and sauté for about 1 minute until fragrant.
Add the seasoned shrimp to the skillet and cook for 2-3 minutes per side, or until they are pink and opaque. Be careful not to overcook the shrimp, as they can become rubbery.
Once the shrimp are cooked, remove them from the skillet and set aside.
In the same skillet, add the spiralized zucchini noodles. Cook for 2-3 minutes, tossing occasionally, until the zucchini noodles are just tender but still have a slight crunch.
Return the cooked shrimp to the skillet with the zucchini noodles.
Add lemon zest and lemon juice to the skillet, and toss everything together to combine. Cook for another minute to heat through.
Taste the dish and adjust the seasoning with salt and pepper if needed.
Remove the skillet from heat and garnish with chopped fresh parsley and grated Parmesan cheese (if using).
Serve the lemon garlic shrimp with zucchini noodles immediately, while hot.

This dish is light, refreshing, and bursting with flavor from the lemon and garlic. It's a great option for a low-carb meal, and the zucchini noodles provide a nutritious alternative to traditional pasta. Enjoy this quick and delicious meal!

Chicken Caesar Salad Wraps

Ingredients:

2 cups cooked chicken breast, shredded or diced
1/2 cup Caesar dressing (store-bought or homemade)
4 large flour tortillas
2 cups romaine lettuce, chopped
1/2 cup grated Parmesan cheese
1/4 cup croutons, crushed (optional)
Salt and pepper to taste

Instructions:

In a mixing bowl, combine the cooked chicken breast with Caesar dressing. Toss until the chicken is evenly coated with the dressing.

Lay out the flour tortillas on a clean surface.

Divide the chopped romaine lettuce evenly among the tortillas, spreading it out in the center of each tortilla.

Spoon the dressed chicken breast onto the lettuce on each tortilla, distributing it evenly.

Sprinkle grated Parmesan cheese over the chicken on each tortilla.

If using, sprinkle crushed croutons over the chicken and cheese.

Season the wraps with salt and pepper to taste.

To roll the wraps, fold the sides of each tortilla over the filling, then roll it up tightly from the bottom, tucking in the filling as you go.

If desired, you can wrap each finished wrap in parchment paper or aluminum foil to make them easier to handle and transport.

Serve the chicken Caesar salad wraps immediately, or refrigerate them for later. They can be enjoyed as a quick lunch, dinner, or snack.

These wraps are versatile, so feel free to customize them by adding additional ingredients such as sliced tomatoes, avocado, or bacon for extra flavor. Enjoy the delicious combination of tender chicken, crisp lettuce, creamy dressing, and tangy Parmesan cheese in these satisfying wraps!

Veggie and Chickpea Curry

Ingredients:

- 2 tablespoons vegetable oil
- 1 onion, diced
- 3 cloves garlic, minced
- 1 tablespoon fresh ginger, grated
- 2 tablespoons curry powder
- 1 teaspoon ground cumin
- 1 teaspoon ground coriander
- 1/2 teaspoon turmeric powder
- 1/4 teaspoon cayenne pepper (optional, for heat)
- 1 can (14 oz) diced tomatoes
- 1 can (14 oz) coconut milk
- 2 cups cooked chickpeas (or 1 can, drained and rinsed)
- 2 cups mixed vegetables (such as bell peppers, carrots, cauliflower, green beans)
- Salt and pepper to taste
- Fresh cilantro, chopped, for garnish
- Cooked rice or naan bread, for serving

Instructions:

Heat vegetable oil in a large skillet or pot over medium heat.

Add diced onion to the skillet and sauté until softened, about 3-4 minutes.

Stir in minced garlic and grated ginger, and cook for another 1-2 minutes until fragrant.

Add curry powder, ground cumin, ground coriander, turmeric powder, and cayenne pepper (if using) to the skillet. Cook, stirring constantly, for about 1 minute until the spices are fragrant.

Pour diced tomatoes (with their juices) into the skillet, and stir to combine with the spices and onions.

Add coconut milk to the skillet and stir until well combined. Let the mixture simmer for 5-7 minutes, allowing the flavors to meld together and the sauce to thicken slightly.

Add cooked chickpeas and mixed vegetables to the skillet. Stir well to coat the vegetables and chickpeas with the sauce.

Cover the skillet and let the curry simmer for another 10-15 minutes, or until the vegetables are tender and cooked to your liking.
Taste the curry and season with salt and pepper as needed.
Serve the veggie and chickpea curry hot, garnished with chopped fresh cilantro.
Serve with cooked rice or naan bread on the side.

This veggie and chickpea curry is delicious, hearty, and packed with flavor. It's a satisfying vegetarian meal that's perfect for a cozy dinner or meal prep for the week ahead. Enjoy the fragrant spices and creamy coconut milk in this comforting curry dish!

Turkey and Veggie Stir-Fry with Peanut Sauce

Ingredients:

For the peanut sauce:

- 1/4 cup creamy peanut butter
- 2 tablespoons soy sauce
- 1 tablespoon rice vinegar
- 1 tablespoon honey or maple syrup
- 1 tablespoon sesame oil
- 1 clove garlic, minced
- 1 teaspoon grated ginger
- 1/4 teaspoon red pepper flakes (optional, for heat)
- 2-3 tablespoons water, to thin as needed

For the stir-fry:

- 1 tablespoon vegetable oil
- 1 lb (450g) ground turkey
- 1 onion, thinly sliced
- 2 bell peppers, thinly sliced
- 2 cups broccoli florets
- 1 cup snap peas
- Salt and pepper to taste
- Cooked rice or noodles, for serving
- Chopped green onions and sesame seeds for garnish

Instructions:

In a small bowl, whisk together all the ingredients for the peanut sauce until smooth. If the sauce is too thick, add water, 1 tablespoon at a time, until desired consistency is reached. Set aside.

Heat vegetable oil in a large skillet or wok over medium-high heat.

Add ground turkey to the skillet and cook, breaking it up with a spatula, until it's browned and cooked through.

Once the turkey is cooked, add sliced onion, bell peppers, broccoli florets, and snap peas to the skillet. Stir-fry for 5-7 minutes, or until the vegetables are tender-crisp.

Season the stir-fry with salt and pepper to taste.

Pour the prepared peanut sauce over the turkey and vegetables in the skillet. Stir well to coat everything evenly.

Cook for another 2-3 minutes, or until the sauce is heated through and the flavors have melded together.

Remove the skillet from heat.

Serve the turkey and veggie stir-fry hot over cooked rice or noodles.

Garnish with chopped green onions and sesame seeds before serving.

This turkey and veggie stir-fry with peanut sauce is packed with protein, fiber, and flavor. It's a satisfying and wholesome meal that's sure to be a hit with the whole family. Enjoy the delicious combination of tender turkey, crunchy vegetables, and creamy peanut sauce!

Broccoli and Cheddar Stuffed Chicken Breasts

Ingredients:

- 4 boneless, skinless chicken breasts
- Salt and pepper to taste
- 1 cup cooked broccoli florets, finely chopped
- 1 cup shredded cheddar cheese
- 1/4 cup grated Parmesan cheese
- 1/4 cup mayonnaise or Greek yogurt
- 2 cloves garlic, minced
- 1 teaspoon dried thyme
- 1/2 teaspoon paprika
- 1/4 teaspoon red pepper flakes (optional, for heat)
- Olive oil, for brushing

Instructions:

Preheat your oven to 375°F (190°C). Grease a baking dish with cooking spray or olive oil.

Use a sharp knife to slice a pocket into each chicken breast, being careful not to cut all the way through. Season the inside of each pocket with salt and pepper to taste.

In a mixing bowl, combine chopped broccoli, shredded cheddar cheese, grated Parmesan cheese, mayonnaise or Greek yogurt, minced garlic, dried thyme, paprika, and red pepper flakes (if using). Mix until well combined.

Stuff each chicken breast with the broccoli and cheese mixture, dividing it evenly among the breasts.

Secure the openings of the chicken breasts with toothpicks to keep the filling inside.

Place the stuffed chicken breasts in the prepared baking dish.

Brush the tops of the chicken breasts with olive oil, and sprinkle with additional salt and pepper if desired.

Bake in the preheated oven for 25-30 minutes, or until the chicken is cooked through and the cheese is melted and bubbly, and the internal temperature reaches 165°F (74°C).

Once cooked, remove the toothpicks from the chicken breasts.

Serve the broccoli and cheddar stuffed chicken breasts hot, garnished with chopped fresh parsley if desired.

These stuffed chicken breasts are delicious served with mashed potatoes, rice, or a side salad. They're perfect for a special dinner at home or for entertaining guests. Enjoy the flavorful combination of tender chicken, cheesy filling, and nutritious broccoli!

Tomato Basil Zucchini Noodles

Ingredients:

- 4 medium zucchini
- 2 tablespoons olive oil
- 3 cloves garlic, minced
- 2 cups cherry tomatoes, halved
- Salt and pepper to taste
- 1/4 cup chopped fresh basil leaves
- Grated Parmesan cheese for serving (optional)

Instructions:

Using a spiralizer, spiralize the zucchini into noodles. If you don't have a spiralizer, you can use a vegetable peeler to create long, thin strips resembling noodles.

Heat olive oil in a large skillet over medium heat.

Add minced garlic to the skillet and sauté for about 1 minute until fragrant.

Add the zucchini noodles to the skillet and toss them with the garlic-infused oil. Cook for 2-3 minutes, stirring occasionally, until the zucchini noodles are just tender but still have a slight crunch.

Add cherry tomatoes to the skillet and toss them with the zucchini noodles. Cook for another 2-3 minutes until the tomatoes are slightly softened.

Season the zucchini noodles and tomatoes with salt and pepper to taste.

Remove the skillet from heat and stir in chopped fresh basil leaves.

Serve the tomato basil zucchini noodles hot, garnished with grated Parmesan cheese if desired.

This dish is light, flavorful, and packed with nutrients from the zucchini and cherry tomatoes. It's perfect for a quick lunch or dinner, and you can customize it by adding protein such as grilled chicken or shrimp if desired. Enjoy the fresh flavors of this delicious tomato basil zucchini noodle dish!

Eggplant Rollatini

Ingredients:

For the eggplant:

- 2 large eggplants, thinly sliced lengthwise
- Salt
- Olive oil for brushing

For the filling:

- 1 1/2 cups ricotta cheese
- 1/2 cup grated Parmesan cheese
- 1 cup shredded mozzarella cheese, divided
- 1 egg
- 2 cloves garlic, minced
- 2 tablespoons chopped fresh parsley
- Salt and pepper to taste

For assembly:

- 2 cups marinara sauce
- Fresh basil leaves for garnish (optional)

Instructions:

Preheat your oven to 375°F (190°C). Grease a large baking dish with olive oil or non-stick spray.

Place the thinly sliced eggplant on a paper towel-lined baking sheet. Sprinkle both sides of the eggplant slices generously with salt and let them sit for about 15-20 minutes. This helps draw out excess moisture and bitterness from the eggplant.

After 20 minutes, pat the eggplant slices dry with paper towels to remove excess moisture.

Brush both sides of the eggplant slices with olive oil and place them on a baking sheet. Bake in the preheated oven for 10-12 minutes, or until they are tender and lightly browned. Remove from the oven and set aside to cool slightly.

In a mixing bowl, combine ricotta cheese, grated Parmesan cheese, half of the shredded mozzarella cheese, egg, minced garlic, chopped parsley, salt, and pepper. Mix until well combined.

Spread a thin layer of marinara sauce in the bottom of the prepared baking dish. To assemble the rollatini, place a spoonful of the ricotta mixture at one end of each eggplant slice. Roll up the eggplant slice tightly and place it seam-side down in the baking dish. Repeat with the remaining eggplant slices and ricotta mixture.

Once all the rollatini are assembled and placed in the baking dish, spoon marinara sauce over the top of each rollatini.

Sprinkle the remaining shredded mozzarella cheese over the top of the rollatini. Cover the baking dish with aluminum foil and bake in the preheated oven for 20 minutes. Then, remove the foil and bake for an additional 10-15 minutes, or until the cheese is melted and bubbly.

Remove from the oven and let the rollatini cool for a few minutes before serving. Garnish with fresh basil leaves if desired, and serve the eggplant rollatini hot.

This eggplant rollatini is a delicious and satisfying dish that's perfect for a special dinner or entertaining guests. Enjoy the creamy ricotta filling, tangy marinara sauce, and tender eggplant in every bite!

Lentil Shepherd's Pie

Ingredients:

For the lentil filling:

- 1 cup dry green or brown lentils
- 3 cups vegetable broth or water
- 1 tablespoon olive oil
- 1 onion, diced
- 2 carrots, diced
- 2 celery stalks, diced
- 2 cloves garlic, minced
- 1 teaspoon dried thyme
- 1 teaspoon dried rosemary
- 1 teaspoon paprika
- Salt and pepper to taste
- 1 cup frozen peas

For the mashed potato topping:

- 2 lbs (about 4 large) russet potatoes, peeled and cut into chunks
- 1/4 cup unsweetened almond milk or regular milk
- 2 tablespoons vegan butter or regular butter
- Salt and pepper to taste

Instructions:

Preheat your oven to 375°F (190°C). Grease a 9x13 inch baking dish with cooking spray or olive oil.

Rinse the lentils under cold water. In a medium saucepan, combine the lentils and vegetable broth or water. Bring to a boil over medium-high heat, then reduce the heat to low and simmer for 20-25 minutes, or until the lentils are tender but still hold their shape. Drain any excess liquid and set aside.

While the lentils are cooking, prepare the mashed potato topping. Place the peeled and chopped potatoes in a large pot and cover with water. Bring to a boil over high heat, then reduce the heat to medium and simmer for 10-15 minutes, or until the potatoes are fork-tender.

Drain the cooked potatoes and return them to the pot. Add almond milk (or regular milk) and vegan butter (or regular butter) to the pot. Mash the potatoes with a potato masher or fork until smooth and creamy. Season with salt and pepper to taste. Set aside.

In a large skillet, heat olive oil over medium heat. Add diced onion, carrots, and celery to the skillet. Sauté for 5-7 minutes, or until the vegetables are softened.

Add minced garlic, dried thyme, dried rosemary, paprika, salt, and pepper to the skillet. Cook for another 1-2 minutes until fragrant.

Add cooked lentils and frozen peas to the skillet. Stir well to combine all the ingredients. Cook for an additional 2-3 minutes to heat through.

Transfer the lentil filling to the prepared baking dish and spread it out evenly.

Spread the mashed potato topping over the lentil filling, using a spatula to smooth it out.

Place the baking dish in the preheated oven and bake for 25-30 minutes, or until the mashed potatoes are golden brown and the filling is bubbling around the edges.

Remove from the oven and let the lentil shepherd's pie cool for a few minutes before serving.

Serve the lentil shepherd's pie hot, garnished with chopped fresh parsley if desired.

This lentil shepherd's pie is a satisfying and nutritious meal that's perfect for vegetarians and meat-eaters alike. Enjoy the comforting flavors of the hearty lentil filling and creamy mashed potato topping!